Genre Fiction

M000234535

Essential Question.
What can we see in the sky?

A Different Set of Stars

by Loretta Wilcox

illustrated by Ann Iosa

"I'll miss you, Muffin," Anita said to her cat. Muffin sniffed Anita's suitcase. Anita was packing. She was going on a trip with her family. A neighbor was going to <u>take care of</u> Muffin. The neighbor liked animals.

> **In Other Words** give food and water.
> En español: *cuidar.*

hairbrush

2

suitcase

Anita had a twin sister named Isabel. Isabel was born three minutes before Anita. The girls were not alike. Isabel was neater. She was bossy, too.

Mom was in the hall. She asked them, "Are you all packed?"

Isabel said, "I am." But Anita was not. Anita's suitcase was a mess!

Anita and Isabel were going to Brazil with their mother. They were going to visit the jungle. Mom was a photographer. She was going to take pictures of the birds that lived there.

The girls were delighted. It was going to be an adventure. They were most excited about staying in a jungle lodge.

STOP AND CHECK

Where does this part of the story take place?

4

bedroom

5

The flight was long, but the twins were excited. Finally, the family arrived at the lodge.

Mom got her camera ready. She was looking for birds to photograph.

lodge

They went to the porch and sat with other guests. Everyone watched the sunset.

The girls sipped fruit smoothies. Anita thought they were delicious.

sunset

Anita leaned back and closed her eyes. She fell asleep and dreamed about her cat.

When Anita woke up, the other guests were gone.

Mom said, "Let's go to our room. We need to get dressed for dinner."

STOP AND CHECK

What happened to change the setting of the story?

camera

8

porch

After dinner, they went back to the porch. It was dark, but they could see by moonlight.

Anita said, "Everything is so different here!"

Isabel said, "No, the moon is the same." Isabel liked correcting Anita.

stars

Anita did not enjoy being corrected. She ignored Isabel and looked for the star pattern she knew. But it wasn't there. She grumbled, "I can't find the Big Dipper."

STOP AND CHECK

What is Anita's problem?

Mom said, "You can't see the Big Dipper here. Brazil is south of the equator." Mom picked up an orange. "Pretend this is Earth. Can you understand why a person here sees a different set of stars?"

Anita imagined herself on the top part looking out at the sky. *It looks different from the bottom*, she realized.

Language Detective	Looks is a present-tense verb ending in s. Find another present-tense verb on page 11.

Now Anita understood. "The Big Dipper is still there. But you can only see it from the other half of the orange. I mean, *Earth*!"

Southern Cross

Mom said, "Right!" She pointed at some bright stars shaped like a cross. "That's the Southern Cross."

Language Detective	Southern Cross is a proper noun. Find another proper noun on page 13.

Isabel said, "I've never seen those stars before."

Anita said, "Well, you've never been on this part of Earth before!"

It was nighttime and time for bed. Anita looked up at the sky. She was happy to see a different set of stars!

STOP AND CHECK

How was the problem solved?

Respond to Reading

Summarize

Use important details to summarize *A Different Set of Stars*.

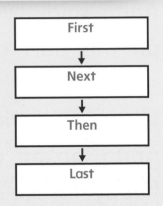

First

↓

Next

↓

Then

↓

Last

Text Evidence

1. How do you know *A Different Set of Stars* is fiction? Genre

2. What happens at the beginning, middle, and end of the story? Use story details to support your answer. Sequence

3. What is the meaning of the word *suitcase* on page 3? Compound Words

4. Write about what the twins see in the night sky at home and in Brazil. Write About Reading

Compare Texts
Read more about stars.

Stars may look yellow, red, blue, or white.

What Is a Star?

A star is a big ball of hot gases. Stars give off light. Their light can be different colors.

17

the Sun

The Sun is a yellow star.

Our Sun

You can see stars at night. But you can see a star during the day, too! That star is the Sun. The Sun looks bigger than other stars. It looks brighter, too. But the Sun is not the biggest, brightest star in the sky. The Sun is our closest star. That's why the Sun looks so big and bright.

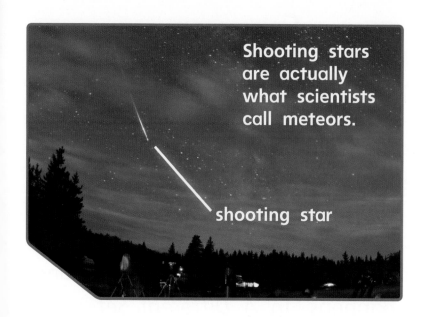

Shooting stars are actually what scientists call meteors.

shooting star

What Is a Shooting Star?

You may see shooting stars dart across the night sky. But these are not real stars. They are pieces of rock or dust. Most burn up before they reach Earth.

Make Connections

What can we see in the night sky?
Essential Question

How are these two texts alike? How are they different? Text to Text

Focus on
Literary Elements

Plot The plot tells the story events in sequence: first, next, then, and last.

What to Look For Look for what the characters do, where they are, and what happens. In *A Different Set of Stars*, twin girls go to Brazil. First, they pack. Next, they arrive in Brazil. Then they cannot find the Big Dipper at night. Last, they learn why the stars look different south of the equator.

Your Turn

Imagine you are writing a story about what people see in the sky. It can be day or night. With a partner, make a chart that shows *First*, *Next*, *Then*, and *Last*. Write one thing that happens in each part of the story.